Easy Business Plan
By Jason Tuller, MBA

Copyright © 2018 by Jason Tuller

All rights reserved. No part of this book may be used or reproduced in any manner without written permission except in the case of brief quotations, attributed to the author, which are embodied in critical articles and reviews.

Table of Contents

Table of Contents
Introduction
Chapter 1 So you want to write a Business Plan?
Chapter 2 Finding Numbers
Chapter 3 Financial Projections
Chapter 4 Who is your Customer?
Chapter 5 Location
Chapter 6 Competition
Chapter 7 Advertising
Chapter 8 The Plan
Chapter 9 The Plan Explained
Chapter 10 Secrets of the Lender

Introduction

Before getting too far into the business plan discussion, it might be good to introduce myself. My name is Jason Tuller and my education includes an MBA as well as further designation as an Economic Development Finance Professional from the National Development Council.

I have worked with entrepreneurs for more than ten years. For more than seven of those years I was a small business consultant who helped clients write business plans. My clients were approved for over $25 million dollars in financing. I worked with over 750 clients, of those there were many people who just had simple questions but more than 200 completed their business plans. Of those, more than 60 were able to start their own business. That doesn't sound like very good success does it? My clients came from all walks of life, some had prepared for decades to own their own business, some were high school kids that wanted to open a shop in the mall. Having a professional help with a business plan does not guarantee that you start a business. Of those who started a business they invested more than $35 million in their businesses. Their businesses employed more than 350 employees. Are there businesses that I haven't seen...yes...but do the concepts contained in this book cover most businesses? Yes they do.

This book will take you step by step through the process of creating a business plan. I explain the research process who/where to ask and how to find information for yourself. I use examples from some of my best and my worst clients. This book also includes a complete example of the written portion of the plan. There are also examples taken from projected financial statements.

Chapter 1 So you want to write a Business Plan?

You have a great idea for a business. Before you quit your job to sell hot dogs on the corner, it important to have a business plan to test out your business idea. You'll want to figure out if you can replace your income and have a successful business before spending any money following your dream. A business plan is not a guarantee that things will be successful, but it is a way to make sure your idea has a chance for success. If, while researching your plan, you find out that the markets for lunches on your corner is only $100 per day and there are three restaurants within walking distance. How would you have enough sales to survive?

A business plan will help you answer many questions. You have to remember that a business plan is not magic and there is no cheap, easy, and fast way to do a business plan. There is a lot of research involved. You'll have to make phone calls and find real world numbers. The more research and time you put in your business plan, the better and more accurate it is. Even a perfectly researched business plan does not guarantee results. I'm sure you have seen businesses start up and several months later the business is closed. Did they have a good or even a great business plan? Perhaps they did. Execution might have been their downfall. Do you have the skills and abilities needed to run the business after the plan is done and financing is secured? That is a question for you to answer for yourself and you must be able to answer that question to anyone investing in your business.

Why do you need to write a business plan? A business plan enables you to see how money flows in and out of the business. The business plan and projected financial statements work together to show your income, expenses, and the timing of those cash flows. Sometimes in a business everything looks great when you look at annual income and expenses, but then you find that when you look at monthly expenses, you run out of cash in the first month and are unable to catch up on bills until the 12th month. An example of this might be a toy store that has 50% of sales in November and December.

A business plan also helps you to explore marketing ideas and costs, your competition, and your business in general. Marketing ideas are fun to think about, but many cost more money than they are worth. Does the $1,000 that you spent on the live radio remote bring in the $10,000 of sales needed to pay for the remote? A business plan helps to get you to think through these scenarios. Your competitors are also factors in your business plan. You need to research where your customers can spend their money on products similar to yours. The business plan also helps you to think through how your business will physically look and how it will function. All of these questions help you to get prepared to run your business in the future.

If a loan is required, the business plan is necessary to take to a lender to get a loan. They require the information in the business plan to be used during their loan committee meeting, where they decide whether or not to give you a loan. Even if you can start your business with cash there are advantages to creating a business plan. You don't want to invest your life savings in a business where you'll lose all your money.

Here's a quick lesson on the brain of the lender. A lender is loaning you someone else's money, they need to be sure of the plan. When you go into a bank and deposit your money in a CD or a savings account, the bank then is able to loan that money out to someone else for their home, vehicle or a business. The interest rate difference between what the bank lends to someone at, and what they pay out on CDs or savings accounts is their profit. They have other ways to profit, but this is a big one for the banks.

The lender needs to make sure you can and will pay back their loan. They also need to make sure that if everything goes bad (your business fails) then they are protected in some way through collateral. They will sell the business assets or collateral to make up their loss. They need to assure the Loan Committee that this is a good loan. They also look at your management capability and ensure that you have a solid plan.

Many of my clients have asked me questions such as, what are the hot businesses to start right now, what are the national trends in business start-ups, or what business will I make money in. I could answer these questions, but they won't guarantee success. You must love the business that you start. You will hate your business just as much as you hate your current job if it is not something that you want to do. You will not be able to wake up at 3 in the morning to go make donuts and be happy about it, unless you love doing it. Your business is up to you, find out what you are passionate about. If you love what you do, you'll never work a day in your life. Find out what you love...then figure out a business around that love. Owning your own business is no walk in the park. You'll work more hours than you can imagine for less money than you need, so loving what you do is very important. Your spouse and your children must also be in favor of starting this business. The more hours you work, the less time you will have to share with them. If they are not in favor of the business, your home life will suffer and if there are problems at home they will transfer to your new business as well. Are you willing to work more hours for less pay than you get now? How are you going to cover health insurance? The answers to these questions and more are the start of your business plan.

Choose your business. If you don't have something specific in mind, the rest of this book won't help you very much. Even if you are not quite sure, just pick one business idea that might work for you and as you progress through this book. Having a concrete example in your mind will help you understand the information needed for the business plan.

Chapter 2 Finding Numbers

Don't get too worried about getting the numbers exactly right. No financial projections are exactly right. Everything changes, but we need to get an idea of how your business is going to function. All financial projections are an educated guess. I won't be talking too much on how to build financial spreadsheets from scratch because to learn those skills takes several different accounting courses and some skill in creating spreadsheets, but I'll explain the concepts in the next chapter. I'll mostly focus on finding the numbers to use in your projections in this chapter.

Even if you are using software such as Business Plan Pro or if you have a professional making your business plan, the plan is only as good as the numbers that are provided. That being said, creating financial projections for a start-up business is many times easier than creating projections for an existing business. If you are purchasing an existing business I suggest getting professional help from an experienced accountant or business consultant. You may be able to find assistance in creating your projections through programs such as SCORE or your local Small Business Development Center (SBDC) http://americassbdc.org/. Their consultants will be able to help you create your financial projections and their services are very handy in difficult cases.

There are a bunch of numbers to gather before you worry about creating projections, though. Don't start worrying about the accounting part before you have found the numbers. It may seem weird to talk about the numbers first, but they take the longest to figure out. It may take a week or more to get a quote from an insurance agent. So start with the numbers and everything else will seem like a piece of cake.

One of the first questions you must answer is, what down payment do you have? That is money that you personally can put into the business. Usually the bank will require you to have some investment in the business. Most will want you to have 20-30% of the total financial investment. That way you have 'skin in the game' and you have a financial stake in keeping the business viable. Sometimes that investment may not be cash. Perhaps you are starting a mechanic shop and have $50,000 worth of Snap-on tools. That has worked for a couple of my former clients. Their wives were upset when they figured out how much their tools were worth, but it enabled them to get loans without having cash on hand.

Your salary is the next item to figure. Many business books will tell you to not expect a salary for several years. That is unreasonable, you need to eat! If you don't take a salary, you eventually end up 'borrowing' money from the business to live on. This is not a good situation. Figure out the salary that you need to live on. The salary must cover the current expenses that your job is covering now. If you don't currently need to work (like a stay at home Mom who is starting a new venture), then in that instance you do not need to put in a salary, but I suggest putting in at least minimum wage or more, just to ensure that your business is going to be able to pay you in the long run. I had one client who started her business thinking that it would just be a hobby so she never figured in a wage in her cost of production. As her business grew, she put in more hours and eventually wanted paid for her time. Unfortunately there was not enough profit margin in her sales to cover her wages, she eventually closed her business. So, be sure that you put in a reasonable salary, even if you don't plan on taking it. Also, remember that you will now have to pay extra taxes (in the U.S.) because you are self employed. Right now your employer, if you are employed, is paying payroll taxes on your wages, when you are self employed, you are responsible for those taxes. If you are just scraping by on your current salary, bump it up by 15 to 20% to ensure that you have enough money for household expenses and taxes. Health insurance and medical costs are a very big cost for many small business owners. If you are starting a business and are going to quit a job where you are provided healthcare, you may be in for a big shock. Many insurance plans are more than $1,000 per month for a family and their coverage doesn't really kick in until $5,000 or $10,000 are spent on your insurance deductible. Add these costs into your salary projection, you never want to start a business that puts your family's health at risk! For my family of 6 my health insurance benefit would take nearly $30,000 to replace.

Monthly Costs are next. As much as you can in this section find real numbers. You can find out rent, utilities, phone, internet, legal, and accounting costs with just a few phone calls. Just a quick note, if a lawyer won't give you a free quote or even a free quick consultation, watch out! They may charge you for every little thing and end up putting you in the poor house. Credit card fees are another expense you need to consider. Many credit card companies charge 3% per transaction or more. I have noticed recently that even franchised stores are using an iPad as their cash register as well as online credit card companies such as Square for their transactions. I actually enjoy Square as a customer because it remembers my credit card and automatically emails me a receipt. I doubt many people think about the customer service aspect of their credit card processor, but if I have a choice, I prefer going to somewhere that takes Square, especially if I am traveling out of town for work. The fewer receipts I have to keep track of, the better my life is. Enough free advertising for them...we've got work to do.

Speaking of advertising, that is another cost that needs to be found. I can't go too deep into advertising here, but there are many books out there to discuss advertising in depth. I also discuss it more in depth in Chapter 7 You can spend as much as you want in advertising, or nothing at all. It is up to you and really depends on your business. If you are in a small town, you may not need to do any advertising at all. You probably will end up spending at least some money on your local newspaper or by buying ads in the school yearbook just to support your community. If you are planning to do newspaper advertising, make a phone call or two to your newspapers to see what ads cost. You might be surprised at how fast they add up. Radio ads can become very expensive very quickly. One of my former client's secretary approved over $10,000 in ads in just a few months. That was an insane amount of advertising for a business that only had a couple hundred thousand dollars in revenue. It didn't end well for the secretary or the business! Remember you have to get value out of your advertising dollars. When you first start up some of that value is just to get your name out there. You like to keep some name recognition going after that, but your advertising dollars must work for you. If you have $1,000 budget for an ad campaign, you need to increase your sales enough to 'profit' at least $1,000 to make that advertising worth it. Right now you just need to get your numbers figured out. Remember, an advertising salesman's job is to sell ads, their job is not to provide you with effective advertising.

Another category of cost is insurance and workers compensation insurance. You can make a quick phone call to your insurance agent for a quote. Don't forget about business interruption insurance. It would be horrible to have a health episode or a natural disaster prevent you from succeeding in your business venture. Also be sure that your business property (building, etc.), business inventory, tools, furniture, fixtures, etc. are covered. Professional service providers also may need some type of errors and omissions insurance.

Office and postage costs are the costs of all of the paper/pens/mail that your business will incur. You will end up spending more than you think on these costs. Most of my clients assumed that they wouldn't spend much on these costs so they put down nothing. I always put at least $50 in these projections, and significantly more if some type of bills need to be sent to customers.

If you plan to own a building or equipment you need to set aside some money each month for repairs and maintenance. It is always sad to see a new business start up and then have outside damage on their building that they don't have money to repair. It makes customers take a second thought about spending their money at that business due to the problems of the building.

Real Estate taxes and personal property taxes are other expenses to budget for. Real estate taxes on properties are pretty easy to find, but you might have to call your state and local department of revenue to find out what your other potential taxes may be.

Payroll is money that you will pay your employees each month. This will include payroll taxes. For example if you plan to hire a full time (40 hours per week) employee at $10 per hour, their pay is $400 per week. You need to budget at least $440 a week just to cover federal payroll taxes and more if there are local payroll taxes. Your own salary does not go in this category, this is only the amount you pay your employees.

Licenses and permits are usually not a monthly expense, but in some cases such as construction businesses permits are a cost of doing business. If you are a restaurant you need to make sure that you have money budgeted for an annual food permit and/or liquor license.

I always include a hundred or two in a miscellaneous category. There are always expenses that you forget to account for.

Computer costs include any monthly fees you may pay for software such as fees for Office 365, virus protection, or design software. Other costs in this budget area would include some monthly set aside for new technology. Unfortunately, computers only last a few years and need replaced periodically.

The travel and entertainment part of the budget include any business costs from business travel or entertaining your clients. If you have any annual conferences or continuing educational needs, this is the category used to budget for those costs. If your business is dependant on wining and dining clients, this category would be used for those expenses.

My projections also contain a column called Other Costs. This would be used for any industry specific costs that might not fit in any of the other categories listed.

Start-up costs would consist of any of the above costs that will be paid before you put the open sign in your window. For example, if you train your employees before opening day, pre-opening advertising, food cooked in chef training, etc. These costs are also costs that won't repeat from year to year, such as utility or rent deposits. Although you will need licenses before you open, I would stick those costs in the first month of operation so that they appear on the next years budget. If you are building a new building, add at least 20% to all construction bids just to cover overages, even if they already put a contingency in the bid. How much inventory will you have on hand? If you are in retail sales, how much (in dollars) will it cost to fill your store? If you are in the restaurant business, how much food do you need on hand? Usually this amount will be 3-8 days worth of food depending on supplier delivery schedules. Maybe less if you are a high-end restaurant specializing in fresh food.

Start-up costs also include the assets that will be purchased. Racks, equipment, tables chairs, shelving, beginning inventory, building, land, building renovation, signage, furniture, fixtures, and goodwill if you are purchasing a new business. If goodwill is involved...don't try to do the financials yourself, call a professional for help. Much of the time when goodwill is involved you are going to overpay for an existing business.

Above all, overestimate all of your costs by 10 to 20 percent.

Once you have all of your costs figured out, the next step is to figure out your sales. Some businesses have a constant flow of cash, other businesses have a cyclical cash flow. An example of this would be an ice cream parlor or an outdoor oriented business. These types of businesses do the majority of their business in the late spring, summer, and early fall. They have very little income in the winter. On the other hand, a toy store does a majority of it's sales in November and December.

There are many ways to try to figure sales. Sometimes your suppliers can provide you with sales projections. Many grocery store suppliers provide information to prospective store owners. You can do some research into the demographics of your area to find out how much money is spent in your industry per person. If you can get a hold of an ESRI report for your locality it will provide a wealth of information like that. Your local SBDC, Economic Developer, or Chamber of Commerce may have access to an ESRI report for your area. Sometimes you just have to do some footwork to find out sales projections. I have sat outside a restaurant to count how many people go in during the dinner rush to see what kind of sales a restaurant had. You can estimate an average check from their menu price then multiply out how many customers to see what their sales look like. If you have a business that is a direct competitor that you can stake out, then take a day or more to count customers, guess how much each customer bought and do some math. You might be pleasantly surprised or you may end up rethinking your business plan. If you have a competitor, do not, I repeat, do not assume you will take any or all of their sales. I had several clients who assumed that they would put their competitor out of business in the first week. They were insane. You might be able to siphon off a few customers, but people are loyal to the businesses that they have used before.

As you can tell, there are many ways to estimate sales. Find one that you are comfortable with and use it to get your estimate. Do not just pick the one that gives you the highest number. You can't expect everyone in town to eat at your restaurant every day for every meal. People just can't afford that. Perhaps there are a couple of people in town that will do that, but not everyone will. You don't want to overestimate sales. Underestimate your sales and compare that to the overestimated costs, if things work move forward with the plan. If they don't, see how many and how big of changes you have to make to get it to work. I'll explain how to do this in more detail in the next chapter.

Another way to estimate costs is to call an existing business in a similar location. Don't call your future competition, call someone in a different but similar sized city. Small business owners love their businesses and they love to tell others about their business. Some will share very specifically with others, while some won't share anything specific. One former client made some phone calls and ended up finding someone who would help train them, and even offered to help them out if they ever got overwhelmed with orders. It was an amazing connection. Be sure not to call people who will be your direct competitors...that is just rude! Call people that are in similar communities more than 50 or 100 miles away and they will be more apt to share with you. Sometimes you also can find information in industry specific magazines or through online forums where business owners chat. I remember gathering a lot of information from a forum for independent pizza restaurant owners. The information is out there, you just have to find it. Remember the more prepared you are when you go into your lender, the more likely you are to get a loan and start your business. If you aren't motivated enough to do the research...will you be motivated enough to do a good job running your business?

I once had a client who wanted to open a candy store in a small town (less than 10,000 people) with little tourism traffic. She thought she could fill a 2000 sq ft store with penny candy and make a living. She was adamant that it was a sound business idea until I got her to estimate her sales in a way that she understood. I asked her if she spent more than most people on penny candy each month, and she said "Yes, I love it". "How much do you spend?" "About $5 per month." "So lets say that a normal candy eating person spends about

$2 on penny candy per month. Then assume that you will get half of the people in town to your store. That means you have about $10,000 in sales per month at a very high estimate." She was trying to keep her prices low, so her cost of goods was at 75%, leaving $2,500 for paying her costs. That wasn't even enough for rent! In order to cover her costs and pay herself a living wage, she would have had to sell $50 in candy to every man woman and child in the town each month! Sometimes you have to go back to the drawing board if your sales cannot support your costs.

Now let's discuss cost of goods. Sometimes this is a difficult concept for people to understand. The easiest way to do this is to start at $1000 in sales. If you know that to have $1000 in sales, you must spend $750 in inventory, that means your cost of sales (or cost of goods) is 75%. Other people calculate by doing a markup which gets a little trickier. For example, you have a $5 widget and you mark it up 50% so you sell them for $7.50. It would be easy to assume that your cost of goods is 50% but it is not, your cost of goods is 66.7%. You take the sales price minus the cost divided by the sales price to get your cost of goods.

It's time for another story again. I once had a couple of clients who were determined to sell food at their restaurant at prices from the 1950's. They had decided that the only reason that restaurant food today is more expensive because of the larger portions offered today. I tried to show them that their sales prices were below even their cost of food. I tried to explain that I would eat at their restaurant every day because they were selling prepared food for less than what it would cost to buy the ingredients. They thought that was wonderful, I would be a customer for every meal. I showed them that they would lose a dollar on every steak...just in food cost. They argued that they would make it up on volume. I tried to explain that if you sold more, you just lost more money. They didn't understand. Finally they got frustrated enough that they left. A little while later a lender called to ask about these clients, they had decided to go straight to a bank. I listened while the lender told me the same story. She couldn't get the clients to understand cost of food either. It was crazy. So, perhaps the moral of the story is that if you can't figure out cost of goods...you shouldn't start a business.

Chapter 3 Financial Projections

This is where I sell my other product, my Easy Financial Projections spreadsheet, sorry for the shameless self promotion. It isn't that expensive and it is well worth the money. It's only 3 dollars if you use the discount code "Ebook" and the spreadsheet will save you hours of building your own spreadsheet. You can follow this link if you would like to purchase the spreadsheet: https://sellfy.com/p/oMn7/ This is the meat of the business plan, financial projections. This is where you input all of the numbers into a cash flow statement and then see if there's a profit at the end of each month and at the end of the year. Sometimes you might be surprised at how just a little change in your projections affect whether or not you can pay your bills. For example, I worked on a plan where we changed the collection period from 60 days to less than 30 and the loan needed changed from almost $200,000 to only $50,000...which is what the bank was willing to loan. These small changes make huge differences in your ability to start and run a business.

Start-up costs would consist of any of the costs mentioned in the last chapter that will be paid before you put the open sign in your window. For example, if you train your employees before opening day, pre-opening advertising, food cooked in chef training, etc. These costs are also costs that won't repeat from year to year, such as utility or rent deposits. Although you will need licenses before you open, I would stick those costs in the first month of operation so that they appear on the next years budget.

Underestimate your sales and compare that to the overestimated costs, if things work move forward with the plan. If they don't, see how many and how big of changes you have to make to get it to work. If you don't like accounting...you might want to close your eyes. There are a lot of numbers coming up. I'll review each financial statement so you can see how they can help you run your business plan. Sometimes lenders will ask questions about the financial statements and if you struggle to answer them that is a clue that you might not be ready for business ownership.

Cash Flow Statement

	START	Month 1
SALES	0	16667
SALES - MEMO	0	16667
CASH IN	0	0
BEGIN CASH	0	65162
CASH SALES(100%)	0	16667
OWNER EQUITY	100000	0
BANK/SBA LOAN	50000	0
TOTAL CASH IN	150000	81829
CASH OUT		
COST OF SALES	0	3333
OTHER COSTS		250
CREDIT CARD FEES	100	250
RENT	0	0
UTILITIES	2000	250
PHONE/PAGER/INTERNET	500	250
ADVERTISING	5000	1000
INSURANCE/WORKERS COMP	500	250
LEGAL/ACCOUNTING	500	50
OFFICE/POSTAGE	0	50
REPAIR/MAINTENANCE	2500	2000
REAL ESTATE TAXES	0	200
PAYROLL	2000	2000
PAYROLL TAXES (7.65%)	153	153
LISCENSES/PERMITS	200	250
MISCELLANEOUS	250	250
COMPUTER	2500	100
TRAVEL AND ENTERTAINMENT	0	100

INTEREST BANK	0	167
SUBTOTAL (EXPENSES)	16203	10903
PRINCIPLE - BANK	0	340
LOAN FEES	1500	0
INVENTORY/SUPPLIES	1235	0
FURNITURE/FIXTURES	400	0
EQUIPMENT/SIGN	10000	0
IMPROVEMENTS	5000	0
BUILDING/LAND	50000	0
GOODWILL	0	0
RENT/UTILITY DEPOSITS	500	0
OWNER DRAW	0	4167
TOTAL CASH OUT	84838	15409
CASH DIFFERENCE	65162	66419

As you can see, the cash flow is a long spreadsheet. It shows how money comes into and flows out of your business. The first column shows what is going on. The second column is labeled START, which is all of the income and expenses that occur before you open your business. Owner Equity is the first part that should have information in it in the second column. It is the cash or other assets that you put into the business. The Bank/SBA Loan shows the amount of the loan that you take out to start the business, the expenses associated with that loan are listed later. Total Cash In shows the total of all the cash that is in the business at the beginning. If you have equipment or something to add to the business, you put the value in as Owner Equity and then you take that same amount out as an expense later.

In the CASH OUT section the first section that has a cost is the Credit Card Fees. That shows the amount that you pay to set up your credit card processing option if you need one for your business. The Rent shows any rent that you need to pay before you open your doors. Utilities shows any utility costs incurred before you open for business. Phone/Pager/Internet shows those costs from before you open your business. Advertising is pre-opening advertising costs. Insurance/Workers Compensation is your insurance costs before opening. Legal/Accounting contains those costs before opening. Sorry, this is very repetitive, but I think you get the point. Payroll taxes are calculated from your total payroll. You may have some bank interest before you open depending on how your loan was set up. The SUBTOTAL (Expenses) row shows the subtotal of all of your startup expenses. The next section starts with Principle - Bank, this lists all of the changes in your assets. It shows your expenses in Loan Fees, Inventory/Supplies, Furniture/Fixtures, Equipment/Sign, building Improvements, Building/Land purchases, Goodwill purchase, Rent/Utility Deposits, and Owner Draw. TOTAL CASH OUT shows the total expenses, it is the SUBTOTAL (Expenses) added to all of the asset expenses. CASH DIFFERENCE is the TOTAL CASH IN minus the TOTAL CASH OUT.

The next column starts with Month 1. It shows all of the income and expenses for the first month of business. It starts out with SALES which is your total sales for the month. SALES-MEMO is the same number. In more complicated situations there would be more information between those two numbers, but if you're in that situation it would be worth it to have an accountant do these for you. BEGIN CASH is the same number that is in the CASH DIFFERENCE row of the Start Column for Month 1. For Month 2, you use the CASH DIFFERENCE row of Month 1 and so on for Months 3-12. Cash Sales shows all of the sales that are cash sales. If you sell on payments (like giving customers 30, 60, 90 days to pay) once again it gets rather complicated, so for this case, lets just assume all of our sales are cash or credit/debit cards.

Now we're getting to the CASH OUT section that shows the expenses for the month. Cost of Sales is the cost of the product you sold during the month. Everything else is just listing the expenses that you anticipate for the month. The asset section gets easier in Month 1. You don't normally spend much on assets in the first month of operation, you should have planned well and purchased all of the assets you need before you open your business. Principle-Bank shows the portion of your bank loan payment that is principle. Interest on your loan is showed in the CASH OUT section. Owner Draw is the salary/wages that you as the owner take out of the business. It is in the asset section because in essence you are taking the cash asset out of the business and putting it into your pocket. Total Cash Out shows the total of all the monthly expenses. Cash Difference shows the Total Cash In minus Total Cash Out. That Cash Difference should be the business 'check book balance' at the end of the month.

The Cash Flow Statement shows how cash flows through your business. It helps to tell you if you can pay your bills. If your Cash Difference is ever negative, that means you are unable to pay your bills. You may find in seasonal businesses that over a year you are profitable, but sometime during your slow times the Cash Difference turns negative which means there will be a point in time where you can't pay your monthly bills. The Cash Flow Statement shows the cash flow during your startup time, each months for 12 months, then it has columns for Year 1, Year 2, and Year 3. Sometimes you will find out that Year 1 is okay because the extra cushion that you put in your loan takes care of extra expenses, but in Year 2 and 3 your cash cushion disappears and your Cash Difference begins to turn negative.

Income Statement

The Business
John Smith

	Year 1		Year 2		Year 3	
INCOME						
SALES	200000	100%	214000	100%	228980	100%
LESS: COST OF SALES	-40000	20%	-42800	20%	-45796	20%
GROSS PROFIT	160000	80%	171200	40%	183184	40%
EXPENSES						
CREDIT CARD FEES	3100	2%	3255	2%	3417.75	1%
RENT	0	0%	0	0%	0	0%
UTILITIES	5000	3%	5250	2%	5512.5	2%
PHONE/PAGER/INTERNET	3500	2%	3675	2%	3858.75	2%
ADVERTISING	17000	9%	17850	8%	18742.5	8%
INSURANCE/WORKERS COMP	3500	2%	3675	2%	3858.75	2%
LEGAL/ACCOUNTING	1100	1%	1155	1%	1212.75	1%
OFFICE/POSTAGE	600	0%	630	0%	661.5	0%
REPAIR/MAINTENANCE	2650	13%	2782.5	13%	2921.6.25	13%
REAL ESTATE TAXES	2400	1%	2520	1%	2646	1%
PAYROLL	2600	13	2730	13	2866	13

		0	%	0	%	5	%
PAYROLL TAXES (7.65%)		1989	1%	2088.45	1%	2192.873	1%
LISCENSES/PERMITS		3200	2%	3360	2%	3528	2%
MISCELLANEOUS		3250	2%	3412.5	2%	3583.125	2%
COMPUTER		3700	2%	3885	2%	4079.25	2%
TRAVEL AND ENTERTAINMENT		1200	1%	1260	1%	1323	1%
INTEREST BANK		1924.461	1%	1755.373	1%	1579.397	1%
SUBTOTAL		1069 63.5	53%	1120 46.3	52%	1173 84.9	51%
DEPRECIATION		0	0%	0	0%	0	0%
TOTAL EXPENSES		1069 63.5	53%	1120 46.3	52%	1173 84.9	51%
OPERATING INCOME		5303 6.54	27%	5915 3.68	28%	6579 9.11	29%

The Income Statement will show you your operating income. Some people would call your Operating Income percent your profit margin. This tells you whether or not your business activities are making money. It takes out the changes in assets and just looks at income and expense. All of these numbers come straight from the cash flow statement. Your Total Sales comes straight over from the cash flow and so do your cost of sales. Then it goes on to your expenses and pulls those over from your cash flow statement. All of the percentages shown are based off of sales. The percentages should roughly stay the same year to year, and if there are wild changes there is probably something wrong with your calculations. Operating Income percentage should increase over time if your sales are increasing faster than your expenses. If it is not, you have a problem and need to lower your expenses or increase your sales. You might have noticed that I skipped Depreciation and there is nothing in the spreadsheet about Depreciation. That is because Depreciation is an expense that is not a cash expense, it is just a calculation for accounting and taxes. Depreciation is a way to claim asset purchases as an expense to reduce your tax liability. It is not something your bank worries about when they are trying to figure out if you have enough cash to pay back your loan, which is why I don't concern myself with it when creating business plans.

Balance Sheet

The Business
John Smith

	START	Year 1	Year 2	Year 3
ASSETS				
CASH ON HAND	150000	80251	81586	85644
ACCOUNTS RECEIVABLE	0	0	0	0
INVENTORY/SUPPLIES	0	1235	1235	1235
FURNITURE/FIXTURES	0	400	400	400
EQUIPMENT/SIGN	0	10000	10000	10000
IMPROVEMENTS	0	5000	5000	5000
BUILDING/LAND	0	50000	50000	50000
GOODWILL	0	0	0	0
LESS: ACCUM DEPREC	0	0	0	0
LOAN FEES	0	1500	1500	1500
RENT/UTILITY DEPOSITS	0	500	500	500
TOTAL ASSETS	150000	148886	150221	154279
LIABILITIES				
OTHER LOANS - ST	0	0	0	0
OTHER LOANS - LT	0	0	0	0
BANK LOAN - ST	4150	4319	4495	4678
BANK LOAN - LT	45850	41530	37035	32357
TOTAL LIABILITIES	50000	45850	41530	37035
EQUITY				
OWNER CAPITAL	100000	100000	103037	108690
LESS: OWNER DRAW	0	-	-	-

				50000	53500	57245
PROFIT Y-T-D			0	53037	59154	65799
			10000	103037	108690	117244
TOTAL EQUITY						
			15000	148886	150221	154279
TOTAL LIAB/EQUITY						

The Balance Sheet is one of the fun accounting sheets that doesn't show much for your day to day operations. It shows only assets and liabilities. These numbers come from the Cash Flow Statement as well. Your asset numbers for START come from your Total Cash In. The Liabilities show your bank loans and other loans that you may have from family or friends. The Bank Loan - ST means Bank Loan Short Term, which shows the principle of your debt to be paid back in the next twelve months. Bank Loan Long Term is the principle portion of your bank loan that will be paid back after 12 months. Owner Capital shows the amount of investment put into the business or earned by the owner. In Year Two you see that this number comes from Total Equity in Year 1. Less: Owner Draw shows the money you have taken out of the business as an owner. Profit Y-T-D comes from the Operating Income box on the Income Statement. You add Total Liabilities and Total Equity up to find your Total Liabilities/Equity which should equal your total Assets if everything is correct in your spreadsheet.

By this point you should have your financial projections pretty much nailed down and have a pretty good understanding of what they mean. After you put all of these numbers into a financial spreadsheet it should give you a pretty good idea of whether or not you will make a profit. Start with your sales, subtract all of your expenses and then you'll see if you have a profit at the end of the month or year, depending on your projection. The financial projections are the hardest part of the business plan and if you've worked on it while you read the book, then you have it out of the way. The rest of the plan falls into place pretty easily from here. Up next is the written portion of the business plan. This is what most people think of when they talk about a business plan. They fail to realize that the most important part of the business plan is the financial projections.

Chapter 4 Who is your Customer?

The next question that needs to be answered is: 'Who is your customer?' Most of my clients said that everyone is my customer. This isn't true for any business, not even the electric or water company. The customer for utilities is the building owner or renter, it is not the children who live in the houses. A restaurant operator may say that everyone is their customer. Perhaps if you lived in a small town and there was no competition you could say that, you'd be wrong, but you could get away with saying it. A restaurant customer has to have an income large enough to cover their family financial needs and still have a bit left over to spend on wants. In a down economy the first expense to be cut is restaurant expenditures because it is considered by most to be a luxury. Why do you need to figure out who your customer is and why isn't 'Everyone' good enough? It is because we are looking to build a marketing plan. If your customer is 'everyone' than 'any and all' marketing should work. That would be easy...but starting a business is difficult and we have to make sure that we are spending our marketing time and money effectively.

So how do you figure out who your customer is? You must start to describe your ideal customer. If your ideal customer is a cowboy boot wearing rancher from western Nebraska, you might find that a local country radio station would be the most effective way to reach them. Ranchers spend a lot of time in their equipment and they listen to local radio to get the current prices of commodities and the local weather forecast. If, on the other hand, your customer is a stay at home mom of 3, you may find your most effective marketing is through social media sites like Facebook. Do not underestimate the power of having up to date and active Facebook page. Not long ago author Jon Acuff did an experiment on his social media pages. He shared the same thing on Instagram and Facebook. He got tens of thousands of views on Instagram, but he got millions of views on Facebook. You will find that in many smaller towns, Facebook use is almost universal and many community events get advertised and word gets spread quickly throughout the community through Facebook posts. Another option is a permission based customer email list which may end up being the most effective marketing tool available to you. You build this list by asking for your customer's email. When they give you permission to email them you have a direct link into their lives. Send an email or two a month, but be sure to offer something useful to your customers other than sales or discounts, send some information that your customers will value. Just remember not to abuse the privilege and be sure to follow regulations about email lists like the Can-Spam Act (not to be confused with canned SPAM a popular meat product in Hawaii). A permission based email marketing list is a huge asset because you control it. A great Facebook page is great, but Facebook is in control of who sees your posts, one change to their news feed algorithm and your posts may not be see by any of your customers.

Back to your customer. Try to answer the following questions about them. What do they do for a living? How much money do they make? Do they have children at home? Children in college? Grown children? Are they retired? What social activities do they participate in? I'll try to explain each question and the meaning of the answers in a marketing context.

Why does it matter what they do for a living? It will help you to determine how to reach your customer through marketing and what industry you need to watch to make sure your customers are going to have money. For example, if your business is heavily concentrated on selling work boots to people who work in coal mines, you need to keep an eye on the coal mining industry and make adjustments when there is an industry slow down coming.

How much money does your customer make? This question can give you a lot of insight into the habits of your customer. If your customer makes minimum wage, then you know that they won't have much extra money. If you are selling them something they need, you should be fine, but if you are selling something they want (think McDonald's or Applebee's) then you need to realize that any disruption in their life will prevent them from buying your product. On the other hand, if you are selling high end wine (hundreds or thousands of dollars per bottle), maybe your customers make $250,000 per year. You have to think about how many people in your community make that kind of money. You might have a handful of people that can afford that, but do those few people spend enough on wine to keep you in business?

Do they have children at home? This information would be important if you sold children's clothing or toys or items that adults with children at home would not purchase. Perhaps you are a kid based restaurant (think Chuck E Cheese's) perhaps you would want to keep track of school activities that might effect your business such as school plays so you can schedule fewer employees or even close when there are large events.

Children in college? Grown children? Both of these answers could be useful in showing how your customer spends their money. Are they forking over $10,000 per year for tuition? That changes a family's budget significantly. Do they have grown children that they spend a significant amount of time and money visiting or are they spending money on grandkids. Are they listening to kids radio because they are taking care of their grandkids all the time?

Are they retired or near retirement? When people retire, their lifestyle changes. Many businesses have a hard time surviving when their customers retire. They have failed to bring in a new group of customers to replace those that retire and no longer spend money like they did while they were working. JC Penney's would be a great example of this, as their customers aged, they failed to bring younger customers in to replace them and they are currently facing bankruptcy. You might notice this with some specialty men's clothing stores.

What social activities do they participate in? Are your customers going to high school football games, are they going to the Elks Club (a social club), are they spending nights out at clubs? Each of these different activities give you a different marketing niche to look at. You could advertise during the radio broadcast of the football game, or in the football stadium. You could learn if there is radio in the background of the Elks Club or become a member to get some advertising in the club or just to meet new people that could become a customer. Perhaps they go clubbing at 3am on Friday nights, perhaps advertising on telephone poles outside the club or on flyers would be more effective.

The more you know about your customer the easier it is to pinpoint advertising opportunities. Each radio or television station can give you specific information about who views each of their shows and how many people view each show. You might find out that all of your customers watch Days of Our Lives at 12:30 (or whatever) and that you can buy a local television ad. Or you may find out that all of your customers work in an office setting and are in their cars on their drive home at 5:20pm which is a great time to hit them with an advertisement for a steak dinner. You also need to understand how far your customer will travel to get to your store. If you are a convenience store that has nothing super unique in it (like a petting zoo, don't laugh there's one in Utah), then people probably won't travel out of their way to visit your store. You should advertise very locally, if at all. Sometimes, your location is all the advertising that you need. It always makes me laugh when I hear advertisements for a convenience store that is more than 100 miles away from where I am. How effective is that ad? Is the store getting their money's worth?

Chapter 5 Location

Now that you have thought about your customer. Let's think about your location. You've heard the phrase, 'Location, Location, Location.' It is true, your location can make or break your business. In the plan be sure to describe your town, the neighborhood (if your town is larger), the foot traffic by your business, the vehicle traffic directly in front of your business, any large local events that would have an effect on your business, and any tourism that may affect you business. In describing your neighborhood, be sure to mention other businesses that draw a large number of people to the area. There is a reason that small stores seem to spring up around big box stores. They depend on the traffic that the big box store draws to the area. Traffic counts can be very important depending on your business model. You might think that your lender is familiar with traffic counts in your area or even about neighborhood events, but still put that information in your plan. Your lender may not be as familiar with the area as you think they should be. I have had lenders that were amazed at the amount of traffic that flowed in front of a business. Your state department of roads would have information on traffic on major highways, some larger street departments in cities may have similar information, too. Foot traffic is harder to come by. Some downtown associations or Chambers of Commerce may have done some studies that provide this information. Worst case scenario, you could just spend a week sitting in front of your proposed business counting cars and people. Or maybe spend a day and get some good friends to also spend a day for you. Buy them pizza or something, it could work. You don't have to have these numbers if you have a solid knowledge of your customer and how to reach them. If you are depending on people dropping by (think tourist trap stores/cafe's) then you need these numbers.

Chapter 6 Competition

Competition is something that must be researched thoroughly. There are two types of competition, direct competition and indirect competition. Direct competition is those stores that sell similar products and services to yours. McDonalds and Burger King are direct competitors...but so are all restaurants. You might argue that Red Lobster and McDonalds are not direct competitors...but they are competing for that same restaurant dollar. People don't put money in their pocket and say this is fast food money and this is sit down restaurant money...they just say it's my going out money. Indirect competition is a business that fights for the same dollar that you are fighting for. For example after people pay their rent/mortgage, food, and utilities, then the rest of their money is up for grabs. They probably have a car payment, a credit card payment, and maybe some medical bills or other items, but perhaps they have a chunk to spend on themselves. Perhaps they buy clothes, fancy shoes, exercise equipment, or they travel. That money is what many, many businesses are going after. You might not think a clothing store, a travel agent, and a sporting goods store are competitors, but they are. They are all competing against each other to get the disposable income of their customers. There's also a bigger competitor...the nothing. Doing nothing is a competitor, people could always stay home and not come to your business. What are you doing to do to bring them into your business?

In this section of the business plan you want to mention your top two to five direct competitors and write a bit about how your business will be different. There is an example of this section in a few chapters. Although I explained above that competition is very complex and difficult, the banker just wants you to make sure that you have thought about your competitors and that you can quickly tell them what will make you different than them and what will give your customers a reason to spend money with you.

As we talk about competition it is a good time to talk about internet businesses. Yes the internet is where everyone shops these days. Your competition must always include the internet. If a person is price comparison shopping, the answer is easy...the internet or Wal-Mart wins...every time. Unless...you can beat them at their own game. For example, purchase off season clothes or school supplies at a steep discount and then resell them. Watch for 'door buster' sales, hold onto the inventory for a couple of months and then mark the products for less that what the current price is. It can be done, but it takes time and planning. I still think it would be insane to base your entire business plan on this...but sometimes insane works. If you are thinking about starting your own online business. Consider this: Opening up a store on the internet is the equivalent of opening your store in a gang infested neighborhood back alley that is filled only with your direct competitors. Why would anyone go to your store and how much excellent advertising are you going to need to get them there?

Chapter 7 Advertising

Advertising, that opens up a whole realm of possibilities. We've talked a lot about advertising within this book so far, so I'll try not to repeat myself. I will stress once again that expensive advertising is not always the best advertising. Just because an ad is expensive doesn't mean that the sales it brings you will be worth the time. To figure out how effective a certain advertising campaign really is, do something like a printable coupon or a special discount if they say they heard you on the radio. Then keep track of those sales. You can then figure out if the margin on those sales covered the advertising dollars that you spent. For example, let's assume that you the products cost you $50 each and you sell them for $100 each. You spend $1000 on a two week radio ad campaign, offering $10 off if they mention the ad. You sold 100 of the items, for sales of $9000 minus the cost of goods ($5,000) is $4,000 in profit margin. Not bad for a $1000 investment. That easily paid for your advertising. Now what if you sold only 10 with the discount, then sales are $900 cost of goods is $500 leaving only $400 in margin, not enough to pay for the ad. Your ad rep may tell you that this experiment doesn't give you the true value of the advertising because keeping your name in the public mind is also of some value.

That is true...but how valuable is it? That is something that depends on your business and location. If you have a location that has good traffic flow from vehicles or from customers going to nearby businesses, then you might not need to have your name out there all the time. If you have to use advertising to get anyone at all to come to your location, then the top of mind or branding advertising becomes very important.

Currently, social media is a great way to stay in people's minds. In my small town, word travels faster through Facebook than anything I have ever come across. Unfortunately you can only control a small portion of the message that goes out through social media. You can control your own posts, but people could be saying bad things about you and you may never see these posts at all. Some business owners choose not to participate in social media for that very reason...they are wrong. If you are on social media, at least you can control some of what is said about you, if you are not on there at all, then you control nothing. Build a Facebook page, send it to friends and family and ask them to invite their friends and family to 'like and share' the page. Then post some decent information about your business and see how many people you reach. Facebook provides businesses a statistics page that shows how many people each post reached and if they interacted with it. It is a pretty nice feature. Each post also shows how many people saw the post. Right now it seems that posts with photos get more views than anything else. You might think that getting a post out to 50 people wasn't that big of deal...but how many people listen to each radio ad that you put out?

There are people who are social media experts who can help you with your social media needs, but if you can carve out a few minutes a week to do social media, it may be worth your time to do it yourself. Just post simple things like sales, specials, and pictures of your store. You'll be amazed when someone else comments about how they love your business. Search online for more social media strategies and you can become an expert in no time...or you'll have enough strategies to keep yourself busy for months.

One item you can advertise is any event or loyalty programs that you have in your business. Take a page out of some of the big box store's playbook, they have some type of timely sales event every month. Think about it...they move from Halloween, to Thanksgiving, to Christmas, to New Year's Eve, to Valentines Day, to Mother's Day, to Memorial Day, to Fourth of July, to Back to School, to Labor Day, back to Halloween. That is almost a sale every month. Some businesses survive on sales every weekend. Just be warned, don't make your business dependant on sales, unless you plan to do that forever. Take a look at JC Penney, they have been based on sales for as long as I can remember and a few years ago a new CEO came in and tried to change to every day low pricing and he almost bankrupted the business. They had trained their customers to only shop in their store when there was a sale, when there was no sale, their customers didn't buy. You don't want to do that in your business. Keep sales rare enough that a sale is a special event.

In the case of professional and service businesses there are several ways to get your current customers to help in attracting new customers. Referral cards are something simple that a lot of owners use. They just hand each client a business card or five to hand out to their friends, maybe include a discount for the first visit on the back. If you want, ask the customer to write their name on the back of the card and give them some type of incentive when one of the cards gets turned back in. Everyone loves cash or a credit on their next bill. Perhaps you have returning customers, try some type of loyalty card. I've even fell victim to a loyalty card at the state fair. If you ate at a certain food vendor 6 times you got the 7th sandwich for free...or something like that. I did it and after 6 sandwiches in three days (lunch and dinner) the seventh wasn't so good...even though it was free. But that loyalty card kept me coming back in a place filled with competition.

While we're talking about referrals...could you please go back to Amazon and leave a review of this book, maybe even share something about this book on Facebook for me. I'd appreciate it!

Remember you are always advertising your business. How you treat people outside of your business has just as big of effect on your business as your customer service inside your business. If you have made a name for yourself in the community as being a jerk...then I can almost guarantee that your business will fail. If you treat people badly...who would want to work for you? If you are a snob...who would want to come in your store? But the reverse is also true. If you are nice and pleasant people will want to come and support your business endeavor. Each interaction with someone is a potential customer or employee for your store. I remember reading on one industry website about how one owner recruited new help. Once a week he would go out to eat at one of his competitors. If he saw any worker that was excellent he would slip them a card saying if you ever have need of a new job, give me a call. He would also leave a large tip if appropriate. He wasn't trying to steal the worker right then and there, but he did leave them with an option, and left a good impression.

So what does this whole advertising discussion have to do with the business plan? Honestly, not much. I have just found that most of the people starting a business for the first time have very little knowledge about advertising and they get taken advantage of by ad reps. Hopefully this section gave you enough information to be aware of advertising expenses and to know that advertising must have some type of return....or why pay for it? If you are looking for more cheap yet effective options for marketing and advertising I suggest looking up any of the Guerilla Marketing books by Jay Conrad. Even the old books are applicable for today, I think I picked up a copy at a book sale for less than a buck and it was still full of great information.

Now that you've read through all of the questions and thought about the information that goes into a business plan, what do you do with it? I didn't talk much about writing the actual plan. It would be difficult to go step by step through writing the plan. It is much easier to provide the following example, and let you adjust the example in a way that fits your business. So take a look at this example and I'll catch up with you in just a little bit.

Chapter 8 The Plan

TABLE OF CONTENTS

Table of Contents	i
Executive Summary	1
Business Description	2
Markets and Competition	3
Advertising and Promotion	4
Financial Data	5
Management Team	6
Investment and Use of Funds	7
Appendix	8

- Amortization
- Cash Flow & Financial Projections
- Resume
- Personal Financial Statement
- Personal Tax Returns

EXECUTIVE SUMMARY

Jason Tuller proposes the start up of the Medicine Man Creek Trading Post. The proposed business will begin in Fall of 2050. The business will be organized as an LLC. The hours of operation will be Monday through Saturday 7am to 7pm. Hours may be extended if business warrants. Medicine Man Creek Trading Post will provide big city variety with small town customer service, a truly unique experience. The main area of the store will offer general merchandise area as well as a coffee shop area.

Total sales are expected to achieve $500,000 in the first full year of operation. To achieve these sales the business will need to average $1,603 in sales per day. Conservative estimates of sales increases show a seven-percent increase in sales; five-percent increase in expenses, and an adequate increase in earnings before interest, taxes, and depreciation to service the debt and provide a good return on investment. By offering quality products and service the market share projection will be achieved. More detailed information is offered in the business plan that follows.

Statement of Purpose:

Jason Tuller is proposing a total investment of $150,000. He anticipates the use of a commercial loan for $130,000 and has $20,000 cash to invest. The monies will be used for the purchase of equipment, inventory, and working capital. The loan will be repaid as depicted in the appendix, Cash Flow Projection, of this plan.

BUSINESS DESCRIPTION

Jason Tuller proposes the start up of the Medicine Man Creek Trading Post. The proposed business will begin in Fall of 2050. The business will be organized as an LLC. The hours of operation will be Monday through Saturday 7am to 7pm. Hours may be extended if business warrants. Medicine Man Creek Trading Post will provide big city variety with small town customer service, a truly unique experience. The main area of the store will offer general merchandise area as well as a coffee shop area.

Medicine Man Creek Trading Post's business combination will enable people to visit the store on a daily basis. The Medicine Man Creek Trading Post will be a unique store. It will have a stock of merchandise on hand including: electronics, some furniture, house wares, appliances, sporting goods, toys, shoes, clothing, dollar store items, a seasonal section, candy, leather rodeo items, and locally produced items. The merchandise on hand will be augmented by a purchasing service, any item will be able to be ordered from the customer service desk. Medicine Man Creek Trading Post will also research providing cellular phones and plans to the area. The coffee shop will draw people in daily and they will sometimes make impulse purchases which will increase merchandise sales.

The following professionals are used by the proposed business for professional advice:

- Ag Oood, Accountant					(555) 555-1234
- Lenny Thelawyer, Attorney			(555) 555-1234
- A. Gent, Insurance					(555) 555-1234
- Aconar Tist, Management Consultant
							(555) 555-1234

MARKETS AND COMPETITION

The Medicine Man Creek Trading Post main market is Anytown, Nebraska. The population is more than 900 people according to the 2010 Census, of this 200 or more attend the Nebraska College of Tin Sculptures (NCTS). The Dean of NCTS has worked extremely hard to expand the college and has gathered the resources to build two new buildings and plans to double the student population in the next two years. This large influx of college students with a great deal of disposable income is a large factor in the local economy.

There are also many local events for both the college and public schools. These events such as horse shows and athletic events bring many people into the town. Local highway 1223 also has 1380 cars and 200 trucks go between town A and town B on a daily basis according to the 2006 Nebraska Department of Roads Map included in the appendix. According to the US Census' County City Data Book Bingo County had $993,000 in food service and accommodation sales in 2002. According to the US Census the 2010 population of Bingo County was 2,863.

The competition in Anytown is limited. There are three competitors in town. Anytown and Country, the local grocery store provides some general merchandise. Big Canyon Soaps' inventory includes some games, toys, and other miscellaneous merchandise. Anytown Flowers also provides some jewelry, greeting cards, and home decorating items.

ADVERTISING AND PROMOTION

The Medicine Man Creek Trading Post will use many different types of advertising. The most effective advertising will come from satisfied customers. As shoppers experience the new store and atmosphere they will tell their friends and neighbors. The façade on the front of the Medicine Man Creek Trading Post will be a western style trading post, this will entice people driving through town to stop by and see what's going on inside.

Advertising will also be purchased in the local newspapers and perhaps in the Big Town Telegraph and the Medium Town Daily Gazette Tribune. Radio ads would also be purchased on an occasional basis. Press releases will also be used to promote special events. Other promotional activities will revolve around the sports activities in Bingo County. A Facebook account will be set up for the Medicine Man Creek Trading Post which will market to people in the area. A website may also be built for advertising purposes and for stock liquidation.

FINANCIAL DATA

The financial projections included in this plan are based entirely on Jason Tuller's research, experience, and future projections. An estimated cash flow statement on a monthly basis for the first year and yearly totals for the following two years are included in the appendix. The sales figures are achievable in the next 12 months. This cash flow projection does not include depreciation and taxes. The owner projects an increase in sales of seven percent and an increase in expenses of five percent per year in years two and three. Projections are found in the appendix of this plan.

MANAGEMENT TEAM

Jason Tuller will be the owner/manager of the Medicine Man Creek Trading Post. He has more than twenty years experience as a cart pusher at La Z Mart in Big Town. In this position he has been observing the management practices and inventory selection of the largest retailer in the world. In this time he has learned about consumer purchasing behavior, returns, discounts, and inventory shrink. Jason also has a background in inventory control. He was Production Planner at a Welding Shop in Crazy Town for several years and one of his responsibilities was inventory accuracy.

Presently Jason works at Business Plan Writers Anonymous. In this position he works with entrepreneurs and business owners to develop business plans and financial statements. He has worked with some businesses in distress, as well as those with expansion plans. He understands the risks and time involved in starting a new business. Jason's education includes a bachelor's degree in Business Administration (Marketing) and French from Bob's Online College and a Master's Degree in Business Administration (MBA) from the University of Bratwurst.

INVESTMENT AND USE OF FUNDS

The investment requirement to fully fund the startup of Medicine Man Creek Trading Post is $150,000.

SOURCES OF FUNDS:
- Financial Institution - $130,000
- Owner's Equity - $20,000

USES OF FUNDS:
- Inventory - $100,000
- Equipment - $25,000
- Working Capital - $25,000

That's it. There's not much to it, is there? There's about 10 pages that are half full. Of course you can write more, especially if you have some extra marketing information or want to add something in an appendix such as a store layout, menu, pictures of the location of your business, etc. The banker only needs enough information to make a decision, he doesn't need to run your business. Now let's go through the plan one page at a time and I'll point out the information that you can just use...and that which you need to make your own.

Chapter 9 The Plan Explained

For the Table of Contents just make sure it fits your business plan. If you use this template, then keep it the same. Notice in the appendix there are several things that every business plan should have including your projected financial statements, loan amortization, your personal resume that shows that you have the skills needed to run the business, a personal financial statement provided by your bank or you can use form SBA Form 413 that shows your personal financial information (it must show your down payment if you have one), also include your personal tax returns for the last 3 years.

Unfortunately everything in the business plan doesn't translate well to an ebook format. The Table of Contents should have the chapter titles on the left side of the page and the page numbers tabbed out closer to the right side of the page, all in alignment. It should look like a Table of Contents from a printed book.

TABLE OF CONTENTS

Table of Contents	i
Executive Summary	1
Business Description	2
Markets and Competition	3
Advertising and Promotion	4
Financial Data	5
Management Team	6
Investment and Use of Funds	7
Appendix	8

- Amortization
- Cash Flow & Financial Projections
- Resume
- Personal Financial Statement
- Personal Tax Returns

The executive summary doesn't change format much from plan to plan. The first paragraph stays the same, just modify it for your business. The last sentence is your value proposition.

The second paragraph outlines your financial information. Listing your total sales for the first year gives your lender a good idea of whether your plan is achievable or not. The second sentence was the same in every business plan I wrote. The third sentence is a restatement of the value proposition. The fourth stays the same.

The Statement of Purpose tells the lender the amount of funding you are looking for. Of course you need to change it to match your plan, but the format can stay the same. If you have a down payment or other types of collateral be sure to mention it here. For example you would say: "He anticipates the use of a commercial loan of $130,000 and will personally invest $20,000 cash (or assets, tools, or whatever you have). The next sentence tells the banker what you will be spending the money on. You don't have to be specific here with dollar amounts, just give the general categories. The last sentence doesn't change assuming you have Cash Flow Projections in the appendix.

EXECUTIVE SUMMARY

Jason Tuller proposes the start up of the Medicine Man Creek Trading Post. The proposed business will begin in Fall of 2050. The business will be organized as an LLC. The hours of operation will be Monday through Saturday 7am to 7pm. Hours may be extended if business warrants. Medicine Man Creek Trading Post will provide big city variety with small town customer service, a truly unique experience. The main area of

the store will offer general merchandise area as well as a coffee shop area.

Total sales are expected to achieve $500,000 in the first full year of operation. To achieve these sales the business will need to average $1,603 in sales per day. Conservative estimates of sales increases show a seven-percent increase in sales; five-percent increase in expenses, and an adequate increase in earnings before interest, taxes, and depreciation to service the debt and provide a good return on investment. By offering quality products and service the market share projection will be achieved. More detailed information is offered in the business plan that follows.

Statement of Purpose:

Jason Tuller is proposing a total investment of $150,000. He anticipates the use of a commercial loan for $130,000 and $20,000 in cash to invest. The monies will be used for the purchase of equipment, inventory, and working capital. The loan will be repaid as depicted in the appendix, Cash Flow Projection, of this plan.

The Business Description page keeps a similar format, but can be expanded considerably. Does the first paragraph look familiar? It is directly copied in the executive summary. It doesn't hurt to repeat yourself. My guess is that even after reviewing your plan, the lender will ask questions that are answered in this paragraph.

The second paragraph describes your business. In the example the Trading Post business isn't very complicated, so I don't explain very much. You don't have to provide much more specific information than what I have unless your business is something unknown. If it is a business plan that is something that your lender is familiar with, don't try to explain too much. If it is a restaurant, explain what type of restaurant, fast food burgers, steak house, Chinese buffet, etc. If your business is a technical service business, such as an engineering firm you might want to explain your business, your service region, and your technical capabilities.

The third section contains the names and phone numbers of your professional advisors. Be sure to contact these advisors before including them in the plan. You never know if your banker knows one of the people you have listed. It would be a sure loan denial if you list your banker's best friend and when he asks about you, the advisor says that they have never heard of you.

Another one of those ebook formatting problems hit this page. On my plans I try to line up the names of the professionals and then tab out a bit to line up their phone numbers. That way everything is nice and clean to look at.

BUSINESS DESCRIPTION

Jason Tuller proposes the start up of the Medicine Man Creek Trading Post. The proposed business will begin in Fall of 2050. The business will be organized as an LLC. The hours of operation will be Monday through Saturday 7am to 7pm. Hours may be extended if business warrants. Medicine Man Creek Trading Post will provide big city variety with small town customer service, a truly unique experience. The main area of the store will offer general merchandise area as well as a coffee shop area.

Medicine Man Creek Trading Post's business combination will enable people to visit the store on a daily basis. The Medicine Man Creek Trading Post will be a unique store. It will have a stock of merchandise on hand including: electronics, some furniture, house wares, appliances, sporting goods, toys, shoes, clothing, dollar store items, a seasonal section, candy, leather rodeo items, and locally produced items. The merchandise on hand will be augmented by a purchasing service, any item will be able to be ordered from the customer service desk. Medicine Man Creek Trading Post will also research providing cellular phones and plans to the area. The coffee shop will draw people in daily and they will sometimes make impulse purchases which will increase merchandise sales.

The following professionals are used by the proposed business for professional advice:

- Ag Oood, Accountant   (555) 555-1234
- Lenny Thelawyer, Attorney   (555) 555-1234

- **A. Gent, Insurance** (555) 555-1234

- **Aconar Tist, Management Consultant**

(555) 555-1234

Markets and competition is where you can let some of your research shine. This section, along with advertising, and the financial projections are usually the weakest part of business plans. In this section the paragraphs and detail are up to you. The more information you put in here, the more your lender knows that you have done your research. I wouldn't go much more than two pages unless you have a very complicated market and extreme competition.

MARKETS AND COMPETITION

The Medicine Man Creek Trading Post main market is Anytown, Nebraska. The population is more than 900 people according to the 2010 Census, of this 200 or more attend the Nebraska College of Tin Sculptures (NCTS). The Dean of NCTS has worked extremely hard to expand the college and has gathered the resources to build two new buildings and plans to double the student population in the next two years. This large influx of college students with a great deal of disposable income is a large factor in the local economy.

There are also many local events for both the college and public schools. These events such as horse shows and athletic events bring many people into the town. Local highway 1223 also has 1380 cars and 200 trucks go between town A and town B on a daily basis according to the 2006 Nebraska Department of

Roads Map included in the appendix. According to the US Census' County City Data Book Bingo County had $993,000 in food service and accommodation sales in 2002. According to the US Census the 2010 estimated population of Bingo County was 2,863.

The competition in Anytown is limited. There are three competitors in town. Anytown and Country, the local grocery store provides some general merchandise. Big Canyon Soaps' inventory includes some games, toys, and other miscellaneous merchandise. Anytown Flowers also provides some jewelry, greeting cards, and home decorating items.

The advertising and promotion section is also normally a weaker section in business plans. In general I would say, the bigger the percentage of your budget advertising is, then the more you write....but also the smaller the budget the more you write. In each case you will need more justification for your budget. Be very specific in where and why you will spend your advertising dollars in a specific area. If you have a very competitive market, that may be your reasoning for a larger advertising budget. If you live in a very small community, that may be your reasoning for a small budget. Just be sure that you explain your reasoning completely in this section. This is the section (other than financials) where lenders ask the most questions.

ADVERTISING AND PROMOTION

The Medicine Man Creek Trading Post will use many different types of advertising. The most effective advertising will come from satisfied customers. As shoppers experience the new store and atmosphere they will tell their friends and neighbors. The façade on the front of the Medicine Man Creek Trading Post will be a western style trading post, this will entice people driving through town to stop by and see what's going on inside.

Advertising will also be purchased in the local newspapers and perhaps in the Big Town Telegraph and the Medium Town Daily Gazette. Radio ads would also be purchased on an occasional basis. Press releases will also be used to promote special events. Other promotional activities will

revolve around the sports activities in Bingo County. A Facebook account will be set up for the Medicine Man Creek Trading Post which will market to people in the area. A website may also be built for advertising purposes and for stock liquidation.

In the business plans that I make for clients the financial data section changes the least. For you, be sure to change the name and make sure that the paragraph matches your assumptions in your projections.

FINANCIAL DATA

The financial projections included in this plan are based entirely on Jason Tuller's research, experience, and future projections. An estimated cash flow statement on a monthly basis for the first year and yearly totals for the following two years are included in the appendix. The sales figures are achievable in the next 12 months. This cash flow projection does not include depreciation and taxes. The owner projects an increase in sales of seven percent and an increase in expenses of five percent per year in years two and three. Projections are found in the appendix of this plan.

This is the section that convinces your lender that you and/or your team have the ability to run the business effectively. If you are the main manager of the operation, here is where you put your qualifications to run the business. Put every bit of your relevant experience in this section. If you are running a retail store and you were once a cashier at Wal-Mart, put it down. Don't make a big deal about it, but put it in writing. If you are dependant on someone else to run your business, or if you have some key employees in a business you have purchased, include them in this section. Be sure to talk to them before putting their name in your plan. You don't want word to get back to their current employer! Don't be as thorough with them, but make sure you get the point across to your lender that the experience needed to run the business is available to you. If you don't have the experience to run the business, and you don't have a key employee that can teach you, you may want to find someone to mentor you. In the past several years the SBA refuses to lend to anyone that is starting a restaurant unless they have management experience (including hiring and firing employees) in a restaurant. If you don't have that experience you need to have someone on your team that does. An alternative to that is working for your competitor. Get your needed experience by working for your closest competitor if they are a large chain store. Restaurants are always looking for help and so are retail stores. Get in there and learn as much as you can as fast as you can. Be a good employee, don't try to sabotage them from the inside, that just isn't nice. The better employee you are the more they will value you and the more they will teach you. Working two jobs for a few months will also get you ready to work that much at your new business. Working at the competition will also give you insights into the industry. It is possible that you start working in a restaurant and find out that it is not all fun and games and there is much hard work and more cleaning than you can handle. That is okay. At least you learned that lesson without going hundreds of thousands of dollars in debt!

MANAGEMENT TEAM

Jason Tuller will be the owner/manager of the Medicine Man Creek Trading Post. He has more than twenty years experience as a cart pusher at La Z Mart in Big Town. In this position he has been observing the management practices and inventory selection of the largest retailer in the world. In this time he has learned about consumer purchasing behavior, returns, discounts, and inventory shrink. Jason also has a background in inventory control. He was Production Planner at a Welding Shop in Crazy Town for several years and one of his responsibilities was inventory accuracy.

Presently Jason works at the Entrepreneur Growth Group. In this position he works with entrepreneurs and business owners to develop business plans and financial statements. He has worked with some businesses in distress, as well as those with expansion plans. He understands the risks and time involved in starting a new business. Jason's education includes a bachelor's degree in Business Administration (Marketing) and French from Jim's Online College and a Master's Degree in Business Administration (MBA) from the University of Bratwurst.

This page is pretty self explanatory. Just change it all to fit your business. Sources of funds are anywhere you are getting start-up money, including your personal investment (Equity), any other loans, or investor funds. Uses of funds should match up to the categories on your cash flow sheet. Anything considered an asset would be listed here, but if it is an expense, just add those things up in addition to the money you need to operate and call it Working Capital. Remember your total sources of funds should equal your total uses of funds.

INVESTMENT AND USE OF FUNDS

The investment requirement to fully fund the startup of Medicine Man Creek Trading Post is $150,000.

SOURCES OF FUNDS:
- **Financial Institution - $130,000**
- **Owner's Equity - $20,000**

USES OF FUNDS:
- **Inventory - $100,000**
- **Equipment - $25,000**
- **Working Capital - $25,000**

That's it you're done with the plan...or you're almost done reading the book. Perhaps some of the most interesting insights are hidden in this last chapter. Keep going!

Chapter 10 Secrets of the Lender

10 Things you should know about your lender, loans, and grants!

1. No lender is going to loan you 100% of your project. They want you to risk something more than your credit. They really want you to put cash into this deal. Normally they would like 20%-30% but they can work with less. They may take collateral like cars and a second mortgage on your home.

2. If you don't have a good to great credit score they are not going to loan you money. If you can't manage your own personal finances...why do you think they would trust you to manage their money? Explainable problems such as medical bills or bankruptcies due to divorce are something that lenders see quite often and they can work around them. Be sure to be very upfront about these problems. If the lender finds out about these things from your credit report, you can kiss that loan goodbye!

3. There are different types of lenders. Large National Banks have very strict lending rules. If you fit into their box, then they are very helpful. At one such bank I had a client whose first language was not English and not widespread in the area, we went into the bank to talk to the lender and they had a translator on the line that worked at another one of their branches. It was amazing. But, if your business does not fit into their box...then you don't get a loan from them. It's not you...it's them. They just can't be flexible because of how big they are. Large local banks is the next type of lender. This is a bank that is the main branch of their bank, and they have other branches in other communities. I have found that these banks can work almost any deal. They would make their decision locally. They also should be familiar with lending with government guarantees such as SBA and USDA. Small local banks would be a single bank with no branches. These can be very good lenders, but they might shy away from bigger loans or loans that need some sort of SBA guarantee.

4. There are other sources of loans. Your lender may not be willing to provide everything you need for your loan. You can use loans from local, regional, or state economic development groups to fill that gap. Almost all of these organizations require you to work with a traditional bank lender in addition to getting their financing.

5. There are a lot of loan options that you can use to get you funded. Do not be outraged if your lender suggests something other than a commercial loan. Sometimes your lender can provide more flexible terms with a simple personal loan backed by your vehicles. You could ask for loans from family and friends (sometimes dangerous, especially if you go bankrupt). Do not fund your business with credit cards. Staying in business is hard enough without paying 18% on your debt....I don't care if you get rewards points for it! There are several types of government guarantees for your loans. These would come through the USDA or SBA. If your lender is looking at one of these types of loans, be sure to ask how long it will take. Some types of SBA loans can be approved in 24 hours or less with minimal paperwork, others take several weeks after you fill out mountains of paperwork. I have heard of some USDA loans taking more than 6 months to get financed. These government loans are a way for a bank to get you financing in the hope that your business relationship is long and profitable for them...they make less on a $100,000 government backed loan than they do on a car loan.

6. A perfect business plan may not get funded. What? After reading this whole book and making a perfect business plan you still might not get the loan, how unfair! Yup. Around half of the clients that I worked with did not get their loans funded. You never know why you get turned down for a loan. Perhaps the bank has a loan out to a competitor. Perhaps they have lent money to a business like yours before and lost money on the deal. I had one community where the banks wouldn't lend money to businesses in their own town. You had to go to a neighboring town to get money. It was crazy. Perhaps you have a new lender and he didn't properly convince the loan committee of the merits of your plan. Any number of things could have happened to your loan, that's why it is important to take your plan to several banks to see what they say. I always told my clients to start with their personal bank and if they say no, then shop around.

7. A bad business plan might get funded. There were plans that I made that I wouldn't have touched with a 10 foot pole that got funded in no time flat. Some of them got funded because of money that either the client or their family had, some got funded because of the assets of the client. I'm almost positive that some got funded

because the banker must have been crazy! I never figured out why lenders decide the things that they decide.

8. Your lender is judging you. Every time you go into the lender's office they are judging you. Be sure that you are dressed nicely, that you are clean, and that you don't smell. I wouldn't say it if I didn't have clients do it. Also make sure that you are prepared with the information they need. Think of this as a job interview. When you take your plan into a bank, call ahead and make an appointment. At their jobs lenders have lots of meetings throughout the day and they normally can't see someone who just walks in off the street. When presenting your plan to a lender, hand them a clean copy of your business plan. Don't staple it and don't put it in a fancy binder. If you do that your lender will just have to rip it apart to scan it at a later time. Remember, your lender has to present your case to a committee, he'll need to make copies of your plan. If it is stapled or in a binder it just adds more work for your lender.

9. Buying (selling) a business. Banks are required to lend based on business tax returns. If you are buying a business and the owner says, sure my tax returns show I don't make anything here, but you should see my house, I have marble floors all paid for from this business. It's a cash business, if you know what I mean. (Yes...I had someone tell me that.) Well, that owner got his money from not paying taxes...now his business isn't worth what it should have been if he would have paid taxes. Banks have to lend based on tax returns. In some cases you can prove better cash flows through discretionary spending, but I suggest getting a business consultant or accountant to help with that. There are free consultants who get funding from the SBA and you can find a local one by searching for your nearest Small Business Development Center or SBDC. There is also an organization called SCORE where people with business experience help small businesses, they could set you up with a mentor with industry experience.

10. Grants. Do not depend/hope/need grants to get your business started. No matter what you read on the internet, there are practically no grants available to start your business. There are no grants from the Federal government to start a business. The only grants I have seen for small businesses come either from State or Local Economic Development Groups. In order to save on costs and

put a barrier up for applicants, some of these organizations charge a fee to cover the costs of the pulling a credit report or criminal history of the applicants. These grants are based on the number of quality jobs created or based on investment in the community. Do not spend money on grant books, grant websites, or grant writing classes. Do not spend money online to apply for grants or for someone to apply for grants for you...those are scams. You might even see advertising for a seminar that guarantees that you get a grant by taking their class. The scam is simple, the seminar costs $500, during the seminar you fill out a grant application and amazingly you win a grant for $100 from the organization putting on the seminar. It is not worth it. A legitimate granting organization will help you through the application process or they will point you to someone that can help you.

Just a few more things before you go. Have someone review your business plan before you give it to a lender. Have them check for typos and to make sure they understand your plan before a lender looks at it. Remember your lender is always judging you, and typos are a bad thing. That's it, so go back and finish your plan and take it into a lender and see what happens. Good luck on starting your business and please, go back to Amazon and leave a review of this book, I would appreciate it!